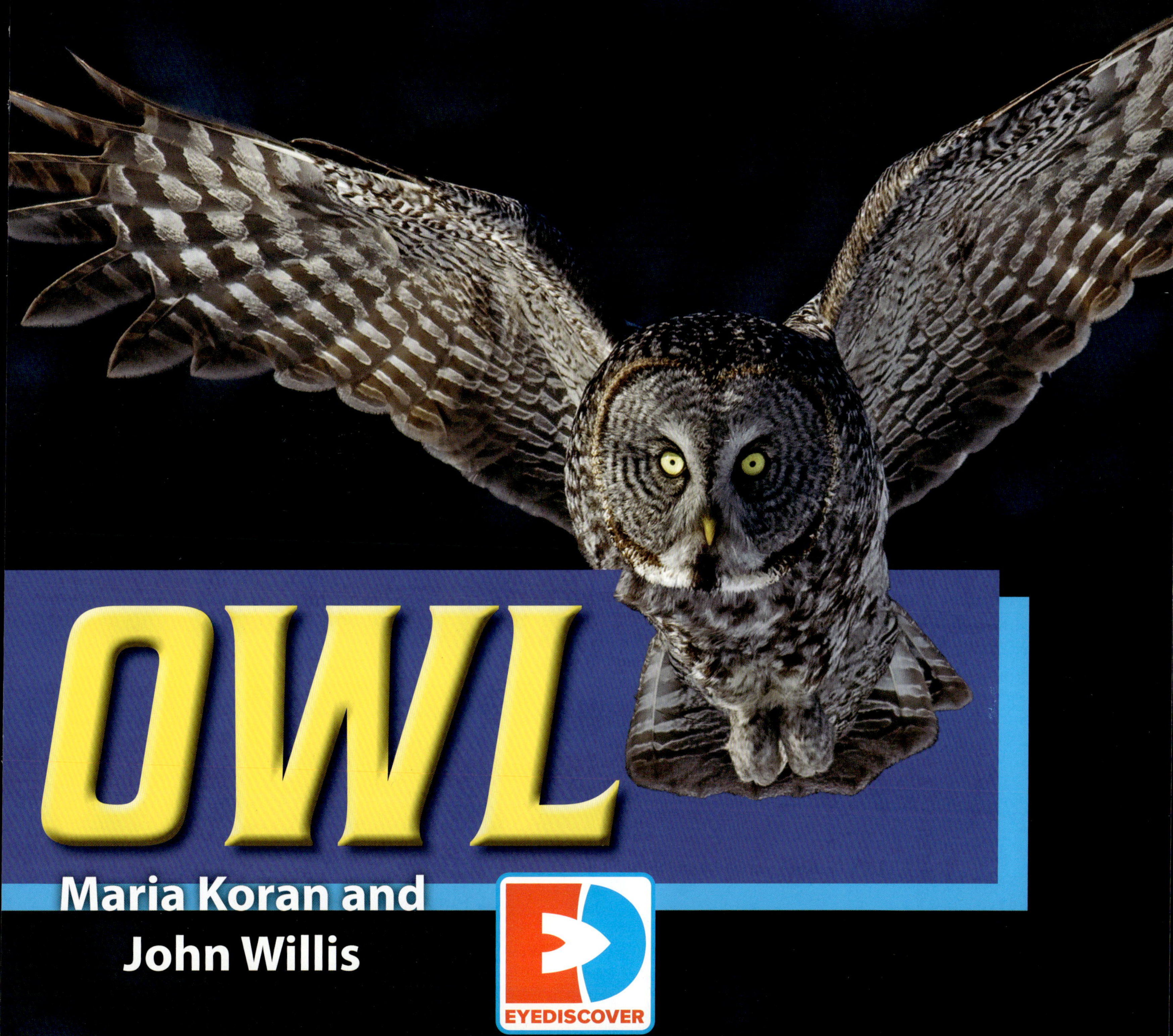
OWL
Maria Koran and
John Willis
EYEDISCOVER

Go to **www.eyediscover.com** and enter this book's unique code.

BOOK CODE

AVN79669

EYEDISCOVER brings you optic readalongs that support active learning.

Published by AV2
276 5th Avenue, Suite 704 #917
New York, NY 10001
Website: www.eyediscover.com

Library of Congress Control Number: 2021937111

ISBN 978-1-7911-4206-3 (hardcover)

Printed in Guangzhou, China
1 2 3 4 5 6 7 8 9 0 25 24 23 22 21

042021
102120

Project Coordinator: John Willis
Designer: Mandy Christiansen

The publisher acknowledges Getty Images, Alamy, and Shutterstock as the primary image suppliers for this title.

OWL

In this book, you will learn about

- what it is
- what it looks like
- how it lives

and much more!

KEY WORDS

Research has shown that as much as 65 percent of all written material published in English is made up of 300 words. These 300 words cannot be taught using pictures or learned by sounding them out. They must be recognized by sight. This book contains 58 common sight words to help young readers improve their reading fluency and comprehension. This book also teaches young readers several important content words, such as proper nouns. These words are paired with pictures to aid in learning and improve understanding.

Page	Sight Words First Appearance
4	all, are, eyes, for, found, large, over, the, their, they, world
7	at, day, food, help, look, many, night, them
8	almost, around, heads, move, things, to, turn, way
11	a, come, different, in, it, white
12	group, is, live, when
15	an, any, let, on, sound, without
16	feet, have, these
19	animals, as, eat, small, such
20	by, can, find, homes, new, people, trees

Page	Content Words First Appearance
4	birds, owls
11	colors, feathers, snow, snowy owl
12	parliament
15	wings
16	claws
19	mice
20	holes